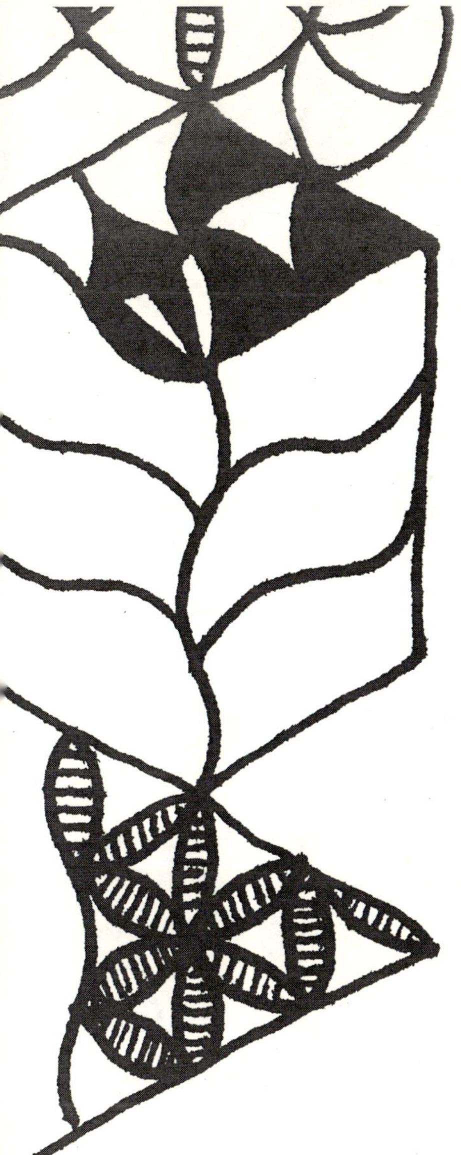

Introduction to

Mindfulness & Manifestation

?

BECOME CERTAIN
about what you want

RELEASE RESISTANT THOUGHTS
preventing what you want from arriving

BE HAPPY WITH IT NEVER COMING,
and never think of it again

Introduction

The only way to manifest is to not care, totally let go, and find another way to feel good and be happy right now. Feel good regardless of your circumstances. You don't need a certain outcome to enjoy this moment. Say, "I don't give a fuck!" to any worries you may have and look around at how awesome *right now* is.

This booklet will help you with each step of the manifestation process. The first three exercises are designed to help you focus on what you want. The next two help you release the resistant thoughts that keep what you want from you. The last two exercises help you feel how you would feel if you got what you want, and then let go of the desire forever. When you let go of any awareness of lack, you'll see what you want is already yours.

Meditation for Manifestation

Breathe in and raise your vibration!
Breathe out and release your resistance.

Breathe in and raise your vibration!
Breathe out and release your resistance.

Relax into this moment right here right now.

Breathe in and be here now.
Breathe out and say thank you for this moment.

Feel gratitude for your health, for your breath, for your friends and your family, for your body. All of this is conspiring to support you and help you and guide you and love you.

Breathe in and listen to your intuition.
Breathe out and release your worries.

Breathe in and open your mind.
Breathe out and release your worries to the ground.

Allow yourself to observe your thoughts. Allow your mind to slow down. Allow yourself to feel your body from within. Relax your body. Relax your mind.

Breathe in and let the flow through you.
Breathe out and let go of your worries.

You can have whatever you want, you just have to let it go. You have to feel as good as you would feel if you had it, and you have to choose that feeling first.

Breathe in and think about what you want.
Breathe out and let go.

Make peace with never receiving this desire. Imagine it's just never going to happen. How can you feel good anyway? How can you not care if you ever get this or not? You can do this by stepping into the present moment, where you already have everything you need.

Breathe in and make peace with what is.
Breathe out and decide to feel the way you want to feel right now.

Whatever it is you want, you want it because it's going to make you feel a certain way. Identify how you want to feel, right now.

Breathe in and feel the way you want to feel
Breathe out and trust in the universe.

Even when you receive that thing you want, it's not going to make you happy. You can only choose to be happy right now. Then you become a magnet to those things you want. But something outside of you will never give you the feeling that you can get from within.

Breathe in and decide to feel good right now.
Breathe out and let your desires go to the universe.

If it's meant to be, it's meant to be. Never think of it again. You have the power to step into this present moment, where everything is fun and there's nothing to worry about. You have the power to relax and enjoy all that you already have. You have the power to quiet your mind and listen, and allow what you want to flow right to you.

1

What Do I Want?

This exercise is designed to help you figure out what you want. What you want will always change, by the day, or the hour, or the minute. And once you get what you want, you'll want something else. Doing this worksheet will keep you busy identifying fresh desires. You can stop thinking about your old stale desires so they can finally manifest.

Once you figure out what you want, you don't have to set goals or timelines or start chipping away at to-do lists. You only have to forget about your desire by finding a way to feel good without it. When you ask, it is given; just trust that the universe is on the case. Keep coming up with fresh desires to distract yourself from the old ones and watch as the old desires manifest faster and faster into your experience.

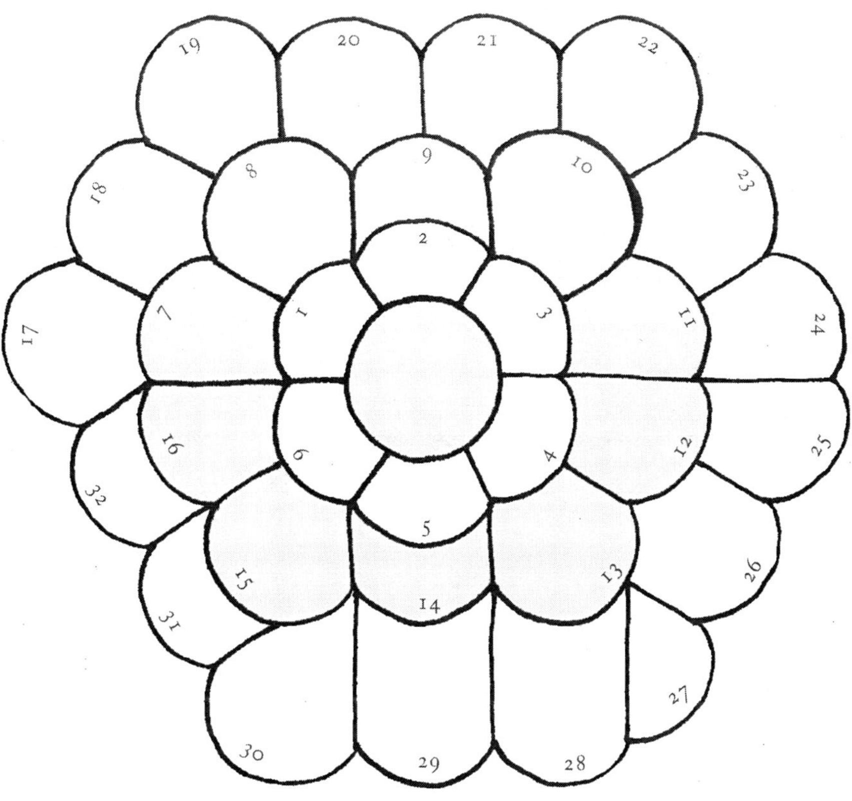

WHAT I WANT TO

1. See 2. Touch 3. Hear
4. Smell 5. Taste 6. Think

HOW I WANT TO FEEL ABOUT MY

7. Body 8. Finances 9. Friends
10. Family 11. Work 12. Thoughts
13. Home 14. Life

DOING

15. What I want to do
16. Where 17. With whom 18. Why

CREATING

19. What I want to create
20. Where 21. With whom 22. Why

WHAT / WHY

23. What or who I want to be
24. Why I want to be that

25. Where I want to be
26. Why I want to be there

27. What I want for my home
28. Why I want that for my home

29. What I want for my body
30. Why I want that for my body

31. Objects I would like to own
32. Why I want to own these objects

2

Best Case Scenarios

Often, we dread the worst case scenario and forget to ask ourselves the best that can happen. As you begin your magickal journey this month, visualize the best possible outcome for each column at the right. Then celebrate! The universe wants that version for you and is conspiring to make it happen.

Identifying the best you can imagine for yourself helps you pulse the signal of having what you want, right now. When you send a signal, the universe reflects that signal. When you feel as if you have something, the universe shows you more evidence. As you imagine each best possible outcome, feel what it would feel like if it came true. In the moment that you feel as if you have it, you already do.

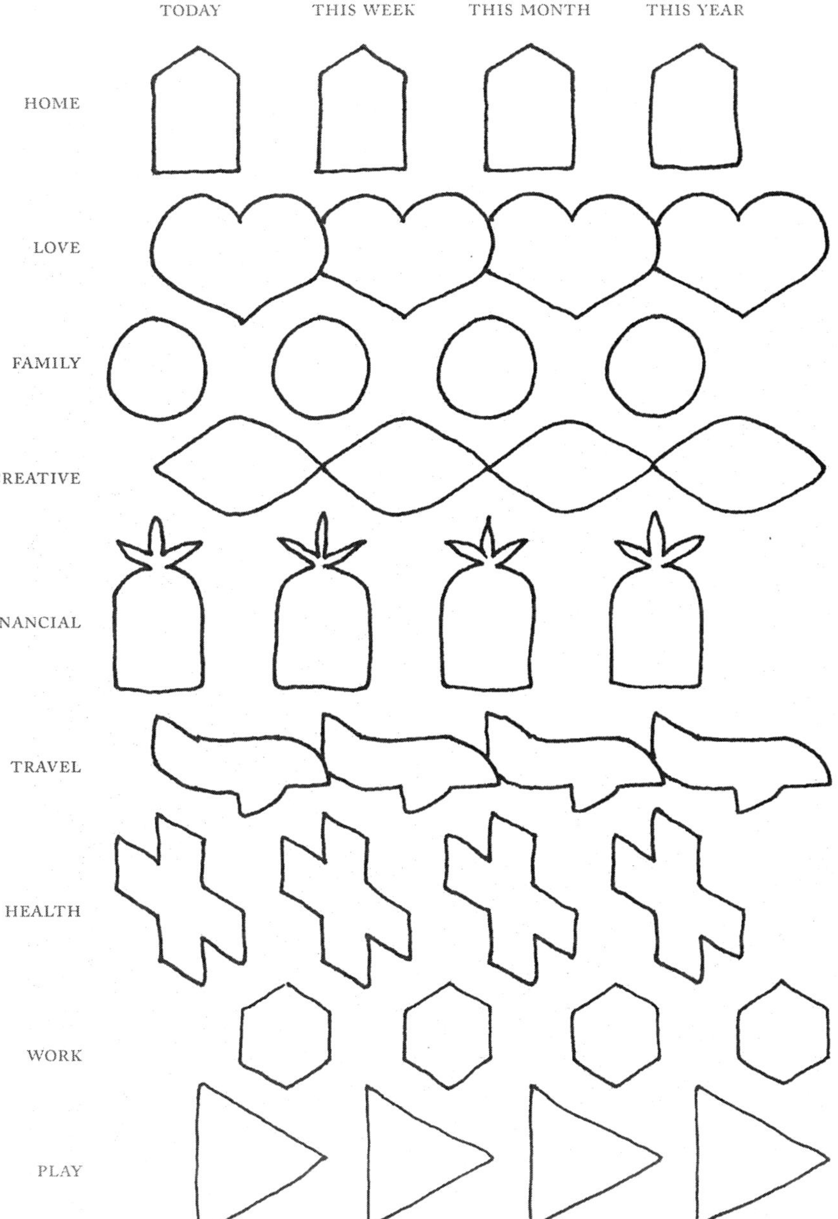
TODAY
THIS WEEK
THIS MONTH
THIS YEAR
HOME
LOVE
FAMILY
CREATIVE
FINANCIAL
TRAVEL
HEALTH
WORK
PLAY

Prepaving

Prepaving is the practice of consciously creating events before they occur. Remembering that we have control over how events unfold can turn nervousness, anxiety, uncertainty or fear into excitement and empowerment. Envision the version you want and celebrate your creation with the knowing feeling of everything going your way.

Before your next meeting, date, or adventure, take a few seconds to think about what you do want, instead of what you don't want.

1. Event title
2. What happens before the event?
3. What's the best that could happen during?
4. How do you want to feel after?

Counting

"When a thought subsides, you experience a discontinuity in the mental stream—a gap of 'no-mind.' When these gaps occur, you feel a certain stillness and peace inside you."

ECKHART TOLLE

~

There's nothing wrong with thinking, but most of us have some thought patterns we wouldn't mind dropping. Focusing on silent counting creates a space in your mind where you can rest.

When you stop thinking, your mood improves.
When your mood improves, the solutions come to you.

Count each shape in the image on the right. Color or mark each one as you go. Focus all of your attention on the numbers, instead of thinking about things in the background.

You will feel a sense of peace overcome you. You will know truths that you cannot define. You will know these truths without ever having to "learn" them.

This feeling is the flow. You allow it when you release resistant thoughts.
Through all your seeking, you will never find it;
it must find you.

5

I Want to Feel Better

This flow-chart emulates a software program. The mind, like a computer, likes to run in loops. When you get caught in a thought-loop, it can be difficult to break that cycle and form a new thought. If you want your mind software to run a different program, you have to write it.

The first step is deciding you want to feel better.

You are only feeling bad because your mind is running in a negative thought pattern. Are you able to shut down the program? Are you able to put the computer of your mind to sleep so it can rest? If so, push the power button and wait patiently for your mind to re-boot. When it starts back up, it will be back in its innate positive thought loop.

If you are not able to force-quit the software, there is still hope. You can train your mind to switch tasks.

Which loop would you like your mind to run? How does this new program feel emotionally and physically while it is being processed?

In the moment that you take the time to imagine a new path for the mind, that path is created. The program is now open, and you can switch to it anytime you please. If you notice yourself fucking around in that old, bad feeling software again, don't worry. You can easily switch back to the most recent version at anytime.

Soon that pesky old version will become completely obsolete.

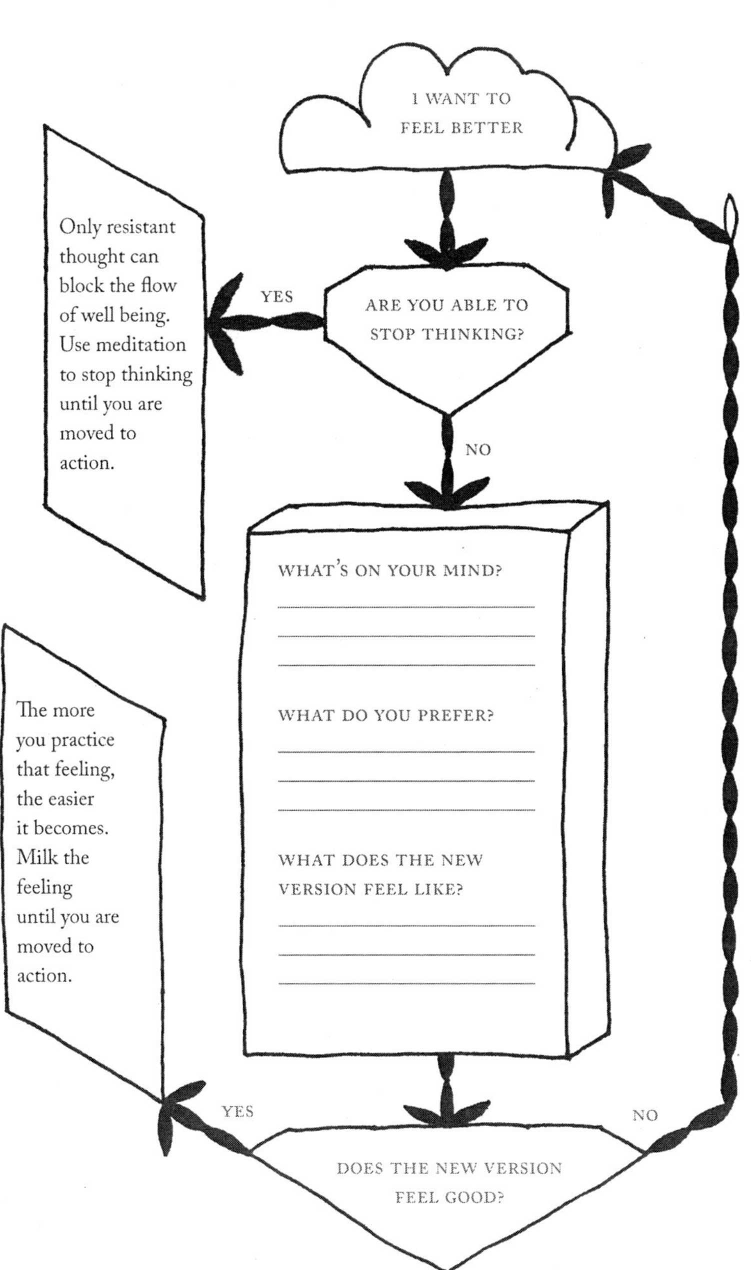
I WANT TO
FEEL BETTER
ARE YOU ABLE TO
STOP THINKING?
YES
Only resistant thought can block the flow of well being. Use meditation to stop thinking until you are moved to action.
NO
WHAT'S ON YOUR MIND?
WHAT DO YOU PREFER?
WHAT DOES THE NEW
VERSION FEEL LIKE?
YES
The more you practice that feeling, the easier it becomes. Milk the feeling until you are moved to action.
NO
DOES THE NEW VERSION
FEEL GOOD?

Life Story

One of the best ways to see what you want in physical reality is to be able to imagine it in your mind's eye. Travel to the future and tell us how your story magickally unfolded just as you foretold.

This is the story of how:

____

1. What was the first indicator the magick was working?

2. Once you began gathering momentum, what evidence did you see that your dream was picking up steam?

3. Everything came together perfectly. Even more perfectly than you ever imagined. As you basked in your manifestation, what was the icing on the cake?

4. How did it feel to get everything you wanted?
Fill in your emotional reaction in the flag at the top.
Choose from the list below or write your own.

Joy
Euphoria
Flow
Inspiration
Appreciation
Empowering
Freedom

Love
Exhilaration
Knowing
Passion
Excitement
Enthusiasm
Eagerness

Happiness
Belief
Optimistic
Hopeful
Content
Relief
Confidence

4.
3.
2.
1.

Plant the Seed

When we experience a particularly emotional chapter in our lives—good or bad, long or short—the tendency of the mind is to replay the event over and over, either trying to resolve a conflict or mining the past for good feelings. Whether you're reliving a positive or negative experience, you are not in the now. You are looking for something outside of this now to make you feel good.

When we are able to stop thinking and be present in the now, we open ourselves up to the best of what we are able to receive. When we stop trying to solve problems or re-create romantic dates, we allow solutions and more dates to flow naturally. When we continue to run things over in our minds, we block the flow of well being and prevent the universe from doing its work.

Name your experience: ______________________________

1. What was the best part of the experience or what is one thing you can learn or take away from it? Write it in the space to the right.

2. Turn this flower you plucked into a present tense affirmation such as, "I let the flow do it," or, "I love it when we get along," or "I feel prosperous." Write the affirmation below the flower. This is your seed.

Now let your seed grow. When you plant something in your garden, you don't turn around the next day and dig it up; you give it time to grow. Give your seed time to grow into more flowers like the one you chose. Anytime your mind tries to revisit this story, say your affirmation to yourself and picture your seed growing. Every time you drop a thought about the past and relax into the now, you nourish your seed.

2. ______________________________

____

____